Animals at Rest

Sleeping Patterns and Habitats

Susanne Riha

BLACKBIRCH PRESS, INC.

WOODBRIDGE, CONNECTICUT

Published by Blackbirch Press, Inc.
260 Amity Road
Woodbridge, CT 06525
web site: http://www.blackbirch.com
e-mail: staff@blackbirch.com

Printed in Belgium

10 9 8 7 6 5 4 3 2 1

First published in German as *Schlaft gut, liebe Tiere* by Annette Betz
Verlag, © 1996.

Library of Congress Cataloging-in-Publication Data
Riha, Susanne.
  [Schlaft Gut. English].
  Animals at rest: sleeping patterns and habitats / by Susanne Riha.
      p. cm.
  Includes bibliographical references.
  Summary: Describes the behavior and habitats of a variety of animals,
with an emphasis on when, where, and how they sleep.
  ISBN 1-56711-425-3
  1. Animals—Juvenile literature. 2. Sleep behavior in animals—
Juvenile literature. [1. Animals—Sleep behavior. 2. Animals—Habits and
behavior.] I. Title.
QL49.R5313 1999   99–25459
591.5'19—dc21   CIP

Contents

Sloth

• • • • • •

It is hot and humid in the rainforest. Bands of brightly colored butterflies flutter through the air. Poison arrow frogs hop along the moist ground. Toucans flap their huge wings at the tops of giant trees. But all this activity goes unnoticed by one animal. Near the top of one tall tree, a sloth is sleeping. He hangs upside down on a branch. He hasn't moved all day. With his long, strong hooked claws he holds onto the branch securely. It seems nothing will stir the lazy creature. Even in the downpour of a sudden thunderstorm, the sloth doesn't move a muscle.

When the sun goes down, the sloth finally moves. Slowly, he turns his head around and grasps some drooping branches nearby. One by one, he pulls the leaves off and stuffs them into his mouth. The leftover raindrops quench his thirst. After a while, the leaves are gone. He crawls upside down along the branches until he gets to a new place with lots of juicy leaves. There, he stops, rests, and hangs. This will be his new spot until night falls again and he has run out of leaves to eat.

Height: 20-24 inches (60 cm)
Weight: 13 pounds (6 kg)
Food: Leaves, soft fruit
Lifespan: Up to 20 years
Habitat: South America, Central America

Orangutan

• • • • • • • • • • • • • •

It is early dawn in the Sumatra rainforest. An orangutan lies sleeping in a nest high above the ground. He has built a kind of platform out of branches, leaves, and palm fronds. He is very comfortable. An elegant pompodaur dove lands nearby. Both the dove and the orangutan love fruit. But this morning, the dove will get a head start looking for food in the forest.

The orangutan is quite at home in the warm, damp rainforest. The many tall trees provide shelter, food, and transportation. With his long arms, the orangutan can climb and swing skillfully from branch to branch. He hardly ever goes down to ground level. When he wants to get from one tree to the next, he swings back and forth. At just the right time, he will let go and fly through the air. As he flies, he grabs a new branch. If he spots a ripe, delicious fruit that is very high up, he may break off a small branch to help him. He will use the stick as a spear or a bat to get at the fruit.

Length: Male: 5 feet (1.50 m) Female: 3.5 feet (1.10 m)
Weight: Male: 200 pounds (90 kg) Female: 110 pounds (50 kg)
Food: Fruit, leaves, insects, bark
Lifespan: Up to 40 years

Clownfish

In the warm waters of the Caribbean Sea, a sea anemone kills fish with its poisonous tentacles. As it does, two orange clownfish swim freely in and out of the anemone's stingers. The clownfish are not affected by the poison and use the anemone for protection. This relationship helps both creatures. The clownfish help to feed their host.

Most often, one male and one female clownfish live in a sea anemone. They catch tiny fish and squeeze them in among the tentacles. That is how both the anemone and the clownfish are fed.

The female clownfish spawns (releases eggs) close to the anemone. By pulling on the tentacles, the female makes the anemone cover the eggs. After hatching, the little clownfish will swim off to find their own anemones.

At night, both clownfish hide themselves within the sea anemone. The tentacles close around them. Like all fish, clownfish sleep with their eyes open.

Length: Up to 4 inches (10 cm)
Food: Small fish
Lifespan: Up to 6 years
Habitat: Tropical seas throughout the world

Pangolin
(Scaly Anteater)

• • • • • • • • • •

The forest floor in southern India is alive with activity. Ants and termites scurry to and from their nests. Rodents dart in and out of tree stumps. In a hole at the base of a rotting tree, a pangolin lies sleeping. Even though it is daytime, he has rolled himself up into a tight ball. In this position, he is safe from danger. He will remain here for the entire day.

The pangolin is covered from head to tail with flat, hard scales. He looks like a round pine cone as he sleeps.

In the evening the pangolin wakes. He begins to move as he thinks about finding some food to eat. He sets off in search of ants and termites. As he walks, his armor makes a clanking sound. When he finds a termite mound or ant nest, he will break it apart with his strong claws. Then he will use his long and sticky tongue to catch insects, larvae, and insect eggs.

Length: 3 feet (1 m)
Weight: Up to 26 pounds (12 kg)
Food: Ants, termites
Lifespan: Up to14 years
Habitat: Africa, Asia

Fennec Fox

• • • • • • • • • • • • •

The Arabian desert floor is burning hot. For months it has not rained. There is not much that can survive in this harsh place. Only plants like cactus—which can store water in their leaves—grow here.

A long-legged roadrunner darts across the sand. With his beak low, he looks for insects. As the bird moves, he comes across a little desert fox. The small animal, now sleeping, dug himself a hole in the sand at dawn. His tough paws protect him against the burning sand, but his thick fur makes him too hot during the day. His extra-large ears help his body get rid of heat, but they cannot keep him cool enough. He avoids the burning sun by sleeping in the shade of his hole. As night falls, the desert cools a great deal. The fennec becomes active. He starts to hunt. Now his thick fur is helpful. It keeps him warm against the cold desert night. Together with other fennecs he catches mice and beetles. With his large ears, the fennec can hear even the smallest sounds. He is even able to detect sleeping lizards in the sand.

Length: Up to 16 inches (40 cm); including tail
Weight: 3.3 pounds (1.5 kg)
Food: Mice, lizards, beetles and other insects
Habitat: Deserts of North Africa and Arabia

Ostrich

● ● ● ● ● ● ● ● ●

During the night, ostriches sleep lying down on the grass. As they do, their long, thin necks are stretched out in front of them. But not all the ostriches go to sleep. Each night, one of them stays on guard until daybreak.

The large birds rise and start moving together. A male leads his hens. With his long neck and large eyes he can see well above the tall grasses. As he leads, he keeps his attention on a group of hungry lions roaming far away. Ostriches will not go where they cannot see what lurks nearby. That is why ostriches avoid forests and swamps.

An ostrich cannot fly, but it can run very fast. And it can cover up to 13 feet (4 meters) in one stride at top speed.

The male leads the group across the plains, searching for grasses and small animals to eat. After a hot morning of hunting, the ostrich flock arrives at their watering hole. Here, they rest and clean before moving on again.

Height: Up to 8 feet (2.5 m)
Weight: Averages 300 pounds (136 kg)
Food: Plants, small animals
Lifespan: Up to 50 years
Habitat: East Africa, South Africa

Leopard

. . . .

In the middle of the hot African day, a leopard lounges in the bushes. Sometimes, he prefers to lie in a cool cave or high in a tree. He will sleep until the sun goes down. He sleeps knowing that no enemies will see him. His spotted fur camouflages him well.

A leopard is every bit as strong as its cousin, the lion. But it is much faster. Leopards like to use surprise in their hunting. He will often jump down from a tree to pounce on his prey. With his powerful paws and strong jaws, other animals are no match for him. He dines regularly on animals that are much larger than he. Antelope, baboons, and water buffalo are a few favorites. On the ground, he can stalk silently through the grass. When he sneaks close enough, he will pounce. Even water is not an obstacle for him. He is a good swimmer.

Once he has his prey, he will take it to a safe place. He may even use his incredible jaws and neck muscles to carry some of his large prey high up—about 15 feet (4-5 meters) into a tree. Once there, he can eat undisturbed.

Height: Up to 2.5 feet (70 cm); shoulder height
Weight: 176 pounds (80 kg)
Food: Antelope, baboons, warthogs, buffalo
Habitat: Africa, parts of Asia

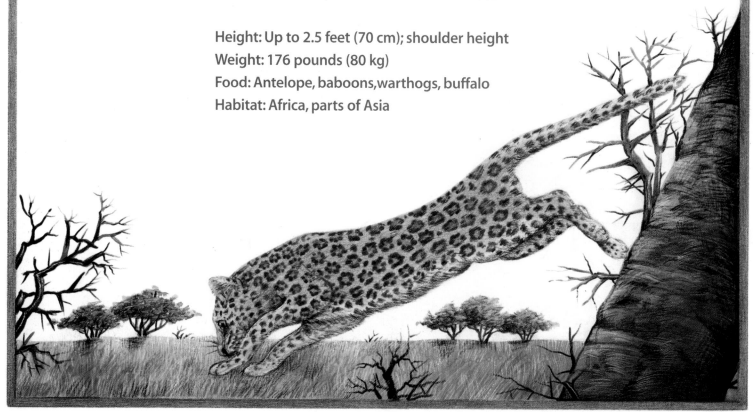

Marabou Stork

In the tall grasses of the African plains (savanna), a marabou stands motionless. Marabous like to sleep standing up. To get ready for sleep, a marabou pulls her head in and blows up her flexible gullet sack with air. This makes a "pillow" on which she can rest her big beak. Even during the day these birds like to take naps. But if there is possible danger, a marabou can become alert in an instant.

Marabous like living near water and often gather there to search for small animals and fish to eat. They are especially fond of young crocodiles and crocodile eggs.

When they stray from the water's edge, the birds walk slowly through the tall grass. As they go, they may follow the tracks of some nearby lions. They do this because the tracks often lead to dead prey that has been left over by the lions. When the marabous find the scraps, they pick the carcasses down to the bones. This is one way in which marabous help to keep the savanna clean.

Height: Up to 5 feet (1.5 m)
Weight: 13 pounds (6 kg)
Food: Carrion (leftover prey), small animals
Lifespan: Up to 20 years
Habitat: Africa, Asia

Koala

• • • • • • • •

The sun beats down on the rugged outback (wilderness) of Australia. In the "fork" of a eucalyptus tree, a female koala rests. Her joey (baby) sleeps with her, clinging to her back. The young koala holds tightly to its mother's fur nearly all the time. That's how it is carried everywhere.

Right now, the joey is still nursing. Before suckling , it crawls around to its mother's front. When it has grown a bit more, the mother will feed her baby pre-digested leafmush. At one-and-a-half years old the young koala will finally get off its mother's back. By then it is almost as big as the mother!

The mother koala is a skillful climber. She moves up and down the trunk of the eucalyptus tree with ease. An adult can eat more than 2 pounds (1 kilo) of juicy eucalyptus leaves each day. These special leaves are the only food koalas eat. And, because the leaves are so juicy, most koalas hardly have to drink anything. In the language of Australia's native people—the Aborigines—koala means "drinks not."

Height: Up to 2.5 feet (75 cm)
Weight: 17.5 pounds (8 kg)
Food: Eucalyptus leaves
Lifespan: Up to 20 years
Habitat: Australia

Fruit Bat

• • • • • • • • • • • •

Bats are nocturnal animals. That means they sleep during the day and are active at night.

The "sleeping trees" of bats are never quite still. Because they sleep while the sun is out, bats will fight for the coolest and shadiest place on a tree. Hundreds of bats may crowd together, hanging upside down from branches. Before falling asleep, they wrap themselves tightly in their wings.

As the sun goes down, a bat colony will begin to stir. As their wings unfold, the tree becomes alive with activity. Together, the bats flutter to fruit trees or bushes. There, they suck the juicy flesh out of ripe fruit. They let the skins and seeds fall to the ground.

At dawn, when the sun begins to rise, the bats swarm back to their resting place. On the way, they will often stop to quench their thirst. They fly in a tight group over the surface of a lake or pond and drink while in flight.

By the time day breaks, the colony is once again hanging on the high branches of its "sleeping tree."

Size: About 8 inches (20 cm), wingspan 47 inches (120 cm)
Weight: About 18 ounces (500g)
Main Food: Ripe fruits
Lifespan: Up to 20 years
Habitat: Throughout Southern Asia

Harbor Seal

· · · · · · · · · · · · · · · · ·

Swarms of sea gulls screech loudly as they fly over the sandbanks. But the sleeping seals nearby pay no attention to their beachside neighbors.

Seals will sleep either in the water or on land. Even when the air or water is cold, seals remain warm. A thick layer of fat under their skin protects them well.

Seals will also sleep underwater. They doze on shallow sand banks, but need to come to the surface from time to time. When a seal surfaces, it opens its ears and nostrils. Then it takes in a full breath of air and dives down again. As it dives, the ear and nose openings close. Seals are champion swimmers. But on land, they can hardly move.

Most seals will hunt both day and night. They spend most of their time looking for crabs and fish. Seals can see very well underwater. When a full moon is out, they can see movement up to 1,300 feet (400 meters) away.

Length: Up to 6.5 feet (2 m)
Weight: Up to 220 pounds (100 kg)
Main Food: Fish, crabs, mollusks
Lifespan: Up to 30 years
Habitat: North Atlantic, South Pacific, North Sea, East Sea

Snowy Owl

The starry Arctic night sky is crystal clear. The air is crisp and very cold. Most animals are tucked safely in their dens, nests, or burrows. They are all trying to stay warm. But the snowy owl is quite comfortable.

In the middle of a frosty field, the snowy owl has found a place to sleep. Her spotted white feathers hide her well in her surroundings. This camouflage protects her from enemies. It also helps her remain nearly unseen while hunting.

This snowy owl, like others, hunts lemmings and voles. These are small, mouse-like creatures that live mostly underground in cold climates.

The female will only nest where there are many voles or lemmings to be found. If she finds enough prey, she will lay up to 10 eggs in her nest on the ground. If food is less plentiful, she will only lay 3 or 4 eggs.

After she has laid her eggs, the mother owl will sit on them to keep them warm. As she does, her male mate will feed her. She has already eaten a great deal in the fall. She stored up enough nourishment to survive for a while in case a snowstorm or dense fog prevents her from hunting during the winter months.

Height: Up to 2 feet (60 cm)
Weight: 4.5 pounds (2 kg)
Food: Lemmings, voles, small mammals, birds
Habitat: Arctic regions of North America, Europe, and Asia

Glossary

Carcass—the body of a dead animal.

Fronds—large divided leaves on a plant such as a fern or palm.

Habitat—the place and natural conditions in which an animal lives.

Humid—damp and moist.

Joey—a baby koala.

Larvae—insects in the stage of development between egg and adult, when they look like worms.

Nocturnal—active at night and sleeps during the day.

Savanna—a flat, grassy plain with few or no trees.

Scales—hard pieces of skin that cover the body of fish, snakes, and other reptiles.

Sea anemone—a sea animal with a body shaped like a tube and a mouth that is surrounded by tentacles.

Spawn—to produce a large number of eggs.

Tentacles—long, flexible limbs of some animals used for moving, feeling, and grasping.

For More Information

Books

Ashby, Ruth. *The Orangutan* (Remarkable Animals). Morristown, NJ: Dillon Press, 1994.

Burton, Jane. *Animals at Rest* (Animal Ways). Danbury, CT: Millbrook Press, 1991.

Feldman, Eve. Mary Beth Ownes (Illustrator). *Animals Don't Wear Pajamas: A Book About Sleeping.* New York, NY: Henry Holt & Co., 1992.

Pfeffer, Wendy. Sylvie Chausse. *Snowy Owls (Creatures in White).* Morristown, NJ: Silver Burdett Press, 1997.

Robinson, Fay. *The Upside-Down Sloth.* Emeryville, CA: Children's Book Press, 1993.

Web Sites

Flying Fox (Fruit Bat)
Learn interesting facts and biological information about these flying mammals by reading the creature profile—www.pbs.org/kratts/world/aust/flyingfox/index.html

Leopards
Discover information on the habitat, behavior, population, and characteristics of the members of the leopard family—www.lynx.uio.no/lynx/catfolk/ssaprd01.htm.

Index